Growing

Andrew Solway

W
FRANKLIN WATTS
LONDON•SYDNEY

First published in 2007 by Franklin Watts

Copyright © Franklin Watts 2007

Franklin Watts
338 Euston Road
London NW1 3BH

Franklin Watts Australia
Level 17/207 Kent Street
Sydney, NSW 2000

Series editor: Sarah Peutrill
Art director: Jonathan Hair
Design: Mo Choy
Photographer: Paul Bricknell, unless otherwise stated
Consultant: Peter Riley
Illustrator: Ian Thompson

Picture credits: Birgid Allig/zefa/Corbis: 16. Maurizio
Brambatti /epa/Corbis: 24. Creasource/Corbis: 26. Julie
Fisher/zefa/Corbis: 10. Andy Crawford: 11l.Chris
Fairclough/Franklin Watts: 22, 25t. Iofoto/Shutterstock:25b.
Liv friis-larsen/ Shutterstock: 7. Owen Franken/Corbis: 13,
27tr. Grace/zefa Corbis: 9. Mango Productions/Corbis: 1.
Bof Mihaela/Shutterstock: 6. Alfred Pasieka/SPL: 27tl. SPL:
12. Luciana Whitaker/Reuters/Corbis: 5.
Every attempt has been made to clear copyright. Should
there be any inadvertent omission please apply to the
publisher for rectification.

With thanks to our models: Isabella Chang-leng, Charlie
Pitt, Eoin Serle and Marcel Yearwood.

A CIP catalogue record for this book is available from the
British Library.

Dewey number: 612.6
ISBN: 978 0 7496 7635 3

Printed in China

Franklin Watts is a division of Hachette Children's Books,
an Hachette Livre UK company.

Contents

The cycle of life

Humans grow and change a great deal during their lives. Each person starts life inside their mother. After nine months or so, a baby is born. The baby grows into a child, then a teenager, then an adult. Adults can produce children of their own. Eventually everyone dies. These changes are known as the human life-cycle.

Try this!

Do you ever measure your height? It's interesting to see how you grow. Sometimes you hardly seem to grow at all. Then suddenly you shoot up quite quickly. Measure your height every month for a year (or more!). Track your changes on a chart.

Measuring your height is a good way to ▶ *track how much you grow from year to year.*

Your height

Everyone grows up differently. Some people become tall and others don't. It's hard to say how tall you might grow. However if there are a lot of tall people in your family, you'll probably be tall as well.

◀ Xi Shun of China is currently the tallest living man in the world, according to the Guinness World Records. He is 2 m 36 cm tall.

Longest-lived people

Studies show that Japanese people are the longest-lived people. They live for 74 years on average. They also have less illnesses than other people. One reason for this is probably the Japanese diet, which is very healthy.

Producing babies

All living things reproduce. Birds, lizards, crocodiles and frogs lay eggs. The eggs hatch into baby birds or animals. Plants produce seeds that grow into new plants. Mammals, such as horses, cats and mice, give birth to live young. Humans are mammals, too.

◀ *Horses are mammals like us. Mammal mothers produce milk to feed their babies during the first part of their lives.*

Human reproduction

Every human has two parents, a father and a mother. We are related to our parents through our genes. We get half our genes from our mother and half from our father.

Billions of people

Humans have been very successful at reproducing. The number of people in the world has grown and grown. In 1800, there were about one billion people in the world. Today there are over six billion people.

Specks of life

Each human being begins life as a tiny egg inside a woman. A human egg is so tiny it is too small to see. You could fit 20 of them across a pinhead.

Fertilisation

Before it can grow into a baby, the egg must be fertilised. This means the egg joins up with a sperm from the father. This happens when a man and a woman have sex together. The fertisilised egg grows inside the mother's womb.

▲ You can often tell that people are related, because they look similar. This picture shows parents with their two daughters.

Inside the womb

As the baby grows inside its mother's womb her tummy stretches to make space for it. It takes about 40 weeks (9 months) for a baby to grow inside its mother.

This shows how a ▶ baby develops inside its mother.

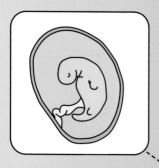

After about four weeks the arms and legs begin to show as tiny 'buds'.
▼

After about 12 weeks the baby is beginning to feel, taste and smell things.
▼

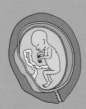

Flexible skull

A human skull is made of several different bones joined tightly together. In a new baby, the skull bones are only loosely joined. As the baby is being born, the bones can move slightly. This makes the birth easier.

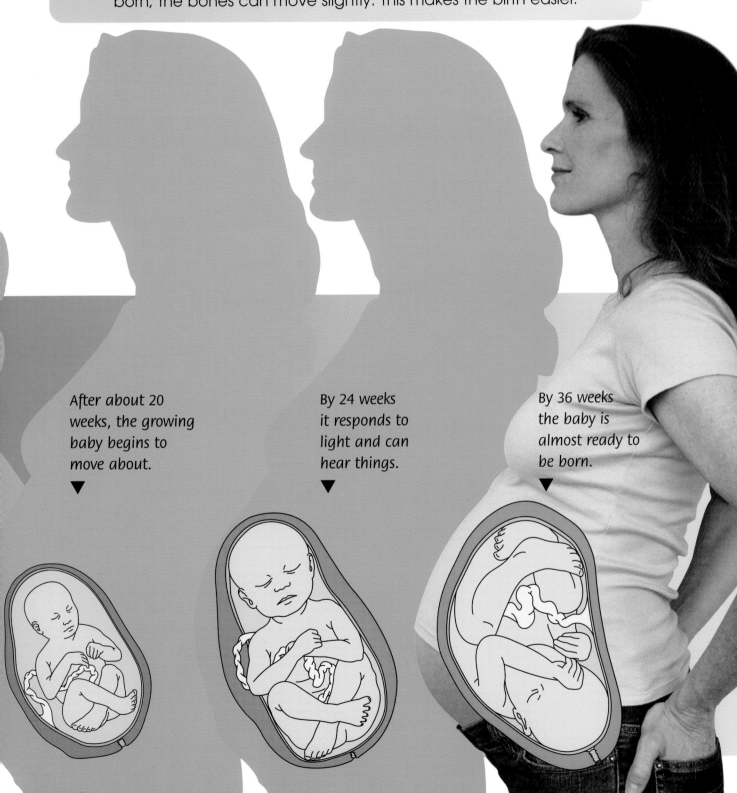

After about 20 weeks, the growing baby begins to move about.
▼

By 24 weeks it responds to light and can hear things.
▼

By 36 weeks the baby is almost ready to be born.
▼

Everyone is different

No two babies
are born the same, and everyone grows and develops in different ways.

Baby weight
Babies vary a great deal in weight when they are born. A very big baby can weigh three times as much as a small one. A small newborn baby can weigh as little as 1,500 grams. This is the usual weight of a bag of flour. A really big baby can weigh over 4,500 grams. This is three bags of flour. Both small and big babies grow up normally.

▲
Babies are weighed and measured regularly, to make sure they are developing properly.

Twins, triplets and more
Most mothers have one baby at a time. However, sometimes two, three or more babies develop inside the mother. Sometimes these babies are 'identical', sometimes not. However, even identical children have small differences between them.

Hair, eyes and skin

Babies may have blonde hair, dark hair or red hair. Their skin could be light or dark. Their eyes could be any colour from light grey to black. We inherit these different characteristics from our parents, through our genes.

Development

There are many other differences in the way that babies develop. One baby may walk at an early age. Another may take longer to walk but be good at learning words. These differences in how we grow carry on throughout our lives.

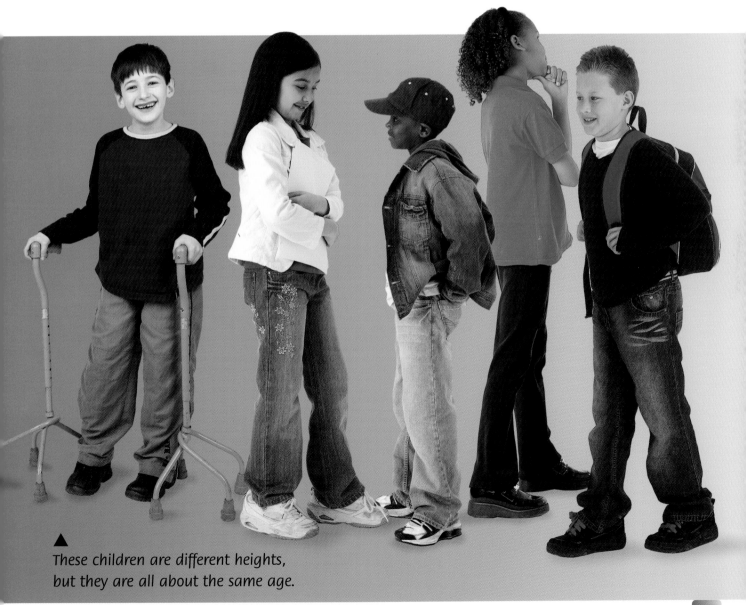

▲
These children are different heights, but they are all about the same age.

A newborn baby

A newborn baby cannot move around. It cannot walk, crawl or even hold its head up. However it can move its arms and legs, and wriggle its body.

Growing bones

We all have a boney skeleton but a newborn baby's skeleton is not all made of bone. Large parts of the skeleton are made of a tough, springy material called cartilage. As a baby grows, the springy cartilage is replaced by stronger, harder bone.

20 years old

13 years old

Three years old

One year old

▲

These X-rays show how bones develop. The springy cartilage (orange and red) is replaced by bone (purple).

When you hold a newborn ▶
baby, you have to support its
head. The baby's muscles are
not strong enough to hold
up its own head.

Eating and sleeping

Newborn babies spend most of their time eating and sleeping. They sleep for over 16 hours a day, in short naps. When newborn babies are hungry they wake up and feed. They cannot eat solid food. They drink milk, either from their mother's breast or from a bottle.

Sight and sound

Newborn babies cannot see very well, but they have a good sense of smell. A baby recognises its mother mostly by smell. Babies cannot talk, but they can make a lot of noise! A baby cries to get the attention of its parents.

Follow the human life-cycle by looking out for these pictures through the book. See how our average height and weight changes as we grow up.

Newborn:
Weight 3.2kg   Length 49 cm
One month:
Weight 4.3Kg   Length 54 cm

From six months to one-year-old

A baby grows very quickly in its first year, getting stronger and developing in many ways.

By six months old a baby has no trouble holding its head up. It can sit and look about, and reach for things that look interesting.
▼

By six months

A baby's eyesight soon gets better, and it begins to look around. At six months most babies are sitting up and reaching for things. They still drink mostly milk, but they may be eating some solid food, too.

At one year

Around a baby's first birthday it will probably be crawling, standing or even walking. One-year-olds can hold a spoon, and are starting to feed themselves. They may also be able to say a few words. A one-year-old baby may weigh three times more than when it was born.

◀ When young children are learning to stand, they will often hold on to something to help them balance.

Getting control

By six months most babies can control their head and arm muscles to look at things and reach for them. By one year old they are able to control their legs and feet much better, too.

Six months:
Weight 7.6 kg
Length 66 cm

One year:
Weight 10.1 kg
Height 74 cm

Toddlers

Babies do not grow so much in their second year. However, their bodies change a lot. As a baby learns to walk, its muscles develop. Its legs and back get stronger, to help it stand upright. By the age of two, babies become toddlers.

Drawing and kicking

As babies grow into toddlers, they learn to control their bodies better. By 18 months most toddlers are beginning to draw with crayons and by two years old they can do things like build a tower of bricks and kick a ball.

▲
This toddler can hold a tiny twig in her hands.

Talking

This is the time when children learn to talk, too. They start talking by listening and copying. Babies say single words first but they soon start putting words together to make two-word sentences, such as 'me drink'.

▶ This toddler is watching his mother's mouth as part of the process of learning to talk.

Talking and the brain

From very early in life, we recognise talking as different from other sounds. The brain has two sides. Both sides process sounds but when we talk or listen to speech, we use only parts of the left side of the brain.

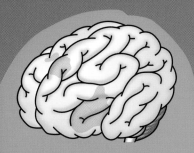

▲ This illustration shows the parts of the brain that are active when we speak. The most active areas (shown darker) are on the left side of the brain.

Two years:
Weight 12.6 kg
Height 92 cm

From toddler to child

At two, children play by themselves. They do not understand how to play with other children. By four they are playing with other children and beginning to make friends.

Becoming independent

By the age of four, children can do many things for themselves. They can climb the stairs, run, throw a ball and ride a tricycle. They learn to dress themselves and wash their hands. Instead of using two-word phrases, they begin to speak properly in sentences.

By aged four children begin ▶ to really enjoy painting.

Brainy children
A child's brain learns and remembers much quicker than an adult's can. A child's brain and body work together to learn balance and co-ordination.

◀ *By the age of four most children are learning to count. However, they do not really understand numbers beyond two or three.*

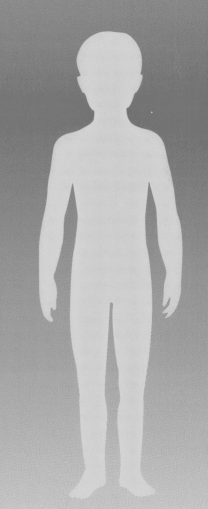

Four years:
Weight 16.5 kg
Height 104 cm

Growing pains
At night, some children get pains in their muscles and joints. These are often called 'growing pains'. Doctors do not think the pains are actually caused by bones and muscles growing. They may just be aches and pains caused by being active during the day. Rubbing the painful area, stretching or putting a heated pad on the part that hurts can often help.

Young children

Between the ages of four and eight, children's bodies take on a more adult shape. A lot more new skills are also being learned.

Changing shape

Babies have a large head and a short body. This is because our brains develop when we are young. As we grow and begin to walk, the body, legs, and arms get longer, so the head seems smaller.

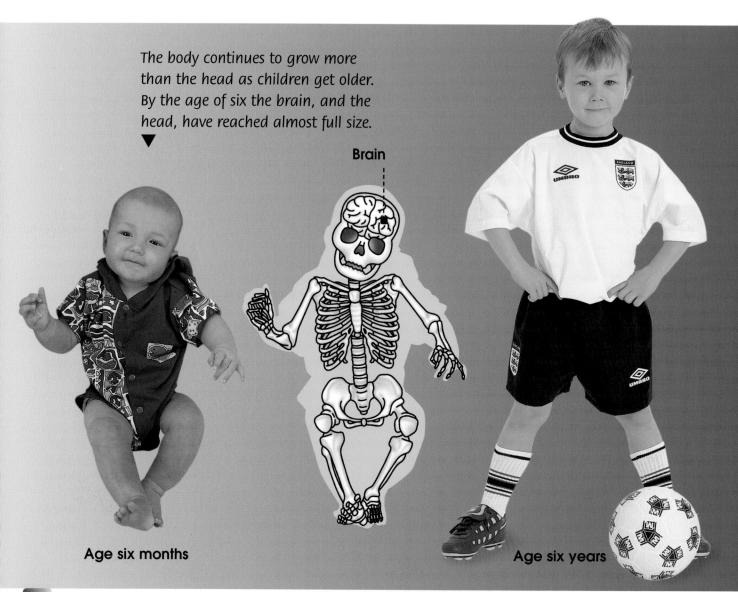

The body continues to grow more than the head as children get older. By the age of six the brain, and the head, have reached almost full size. ▼

Brain

Age six months

Age six years

In the brain

By six or seven most children can read and write. From age four to six, the part of the brain to do with language grows quickly. This is the best time to learn new languages. After the age of 12 we find learning a new language much harder.

◄ *Most children like to have stories read to them from an early age. By the age of six or seven, they can read for themselves, too.*

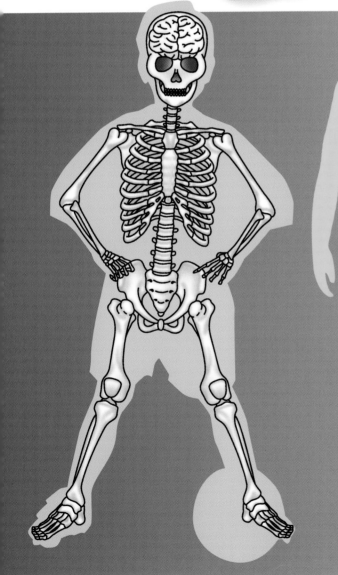

Six years:
Weight 21.9 kg
Height 116 cm

Eight years:
Weight 27.3 kg
Height 128 cm

From child to adult

From about nine years old, young people begin to change from children to adults. This change is called puberty.

Growth spurt

The first sign of puberty is a growth spurt. The hands and feet grow first, then the arms and legs, and finally the body. Girls have this growth spurt before boys. Many girls reach their full height by 13. Boys often carry on growing into their late teens, and generally end up being taller than girls.

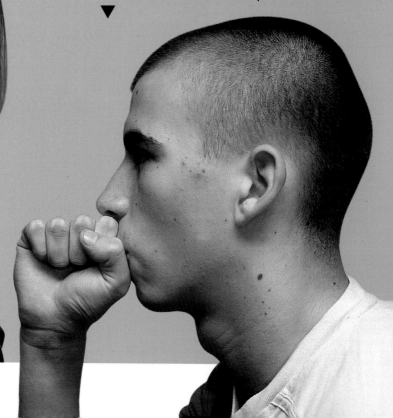

◀ The hormones produced during puberty can affect young people's emotions as well as their bodies. Teenagers can sometimes get depressed or angry for no obvious reason.

One change that happens in boys is that their 'Adam's apple' (the lump in their throat) gets bigger. This change makes them have a deeper voice.
▼

What starts puberty?

The change from child to adult is started by special substances in the body called hormones. A hormone is a substance that is produced in one part of the body and released into the blood. It then travels round in the blood and affects other parts of the body. The hormone that starts off puberty is made by the pituitary gland, which is in the brain.

Male and female changes

Other changes happen in puberty, too. Girls' hips get wider, and their breasts grow. Boys' voices get deeper, and hair begins to grow on their face. As well as growing taller, boys get broader and more muscular.

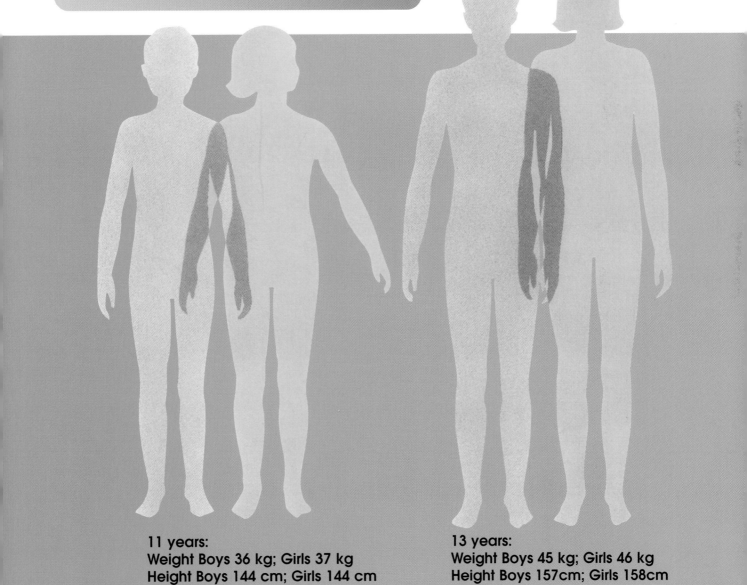

11 years:
Weight Boys 36 kg; Girls 37 kg
Height Boys 144 cm; Girls 144 cm

13 years:
Weight Boys 45 kg; Girls 46 kg
Height Boys 157cm; Girls 158cm

Fully grown

Men and women grow to their full height in their late teens, but the body never really stops changing. Everyone matures differently so there is no set age when we are fully grown.

Muscle changes

Physically, teenagers and young adults are at their peak. In late puberty, bones get stronger. There is also a 'strength spurt', especially in young men, when the muscles grow quickly.

Most of the world's top sportspeople are in their teens or twenties.

▼

Starting a family
As soon as we go through puberty we are able to have children, but most people don't start a family until they are older.

Bulging brains
From the age of 12 to about 18, the front part of the brain enlarges. This is the thinking part of the brain. It is an important time for learning and organising new information. The knowledge and skills young people learn at this time become 'hard-wired'. They become a permanent part of the brain.

The changes in their brains make young adults good at learning and at organising new information. They are at the best stage in their life to face new challenges.
▼

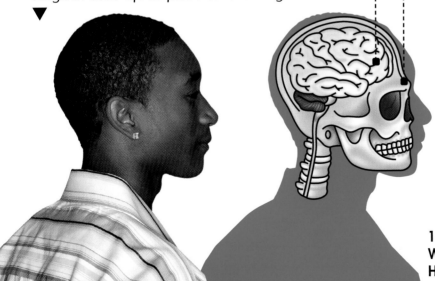

Skull

Front of brain

18 years:
Weight Men: 80 kg; Women: 67 kg
Height Men: 175 cm; Women: 161 cm

Keeping healthy

The best way to be healthy when you are older is to be active and eat a well-balanced diet throughout your life. This will help you stay healthy on the inside and out!

Your food

Eat at least five portions of fresh fruit and vegetables a day. This will give you important vitamins and minerals, and plenty of fibre. Try not to eat too many sweet or fatty foods.

If you eat healthy food all your life, you are more likely to stay healthy into old age.
▼

Keep active

Keeping active is also important. Cycling, hiking, swimming and dancing are all good ways to keep your bones and muscles strong.

Use your brain

It is also important to keep the brain active. Learning new things and solving problems will help you to keep the brain ticking over. If you look after your body and your mind, you have a better chance of having a healthy old age.

Still going strong

Some people keep going strong well into old age. Australian Cliff Young won a long-distance race from Sydney to Melbourne when he was 61. The author Mary Wesley wrote her first book when she was 70. And at 88, US politician 'Granny D' Haddock walked across the USA.

Cycling is good exercise for people of all ages.
▼

Glossary

cartilage
A strong, springy material that makes up some parts of the skeleton. As we grow, some of the cartilage in the skeleton is replaced by bone.

diet
Everything that we eat.

fertilised
When a woman's egg is fertilised by a man's sperm, it starts to grow and develop into a baby.

genes
Substances inside our bodies that act as an 'instruction book' for how we develop and grow. Genes are passed on from parents to their children.

growth spurt
A time during puberty when young people grow very quickly.

hormones
A substance that is produced in one part of the body and released into the blood. It then travels round in the blood and affects other parts of the body.

human life-cycle
The changes in a person's life as they are born, grow into adults and then have babies of their own.

identical
Identical twins or triplets occur when the fertilised egg splits in half, or in three parts, so that two or three babies develop inside the mother. They will all be the same sex and look very similar.

minerals
Simple chemicals such as iron and calcium, which we need in our diet.

puberty
A period from about nine years old, when young people begin to change from children into adults.

responsibilities
Duties that we have, for example adults have a responsibility to make sure that their children are properly looked after.

sex
When a man and a woman have

a special cuddle which may make a baby.

skeleton
The framework of bones that supports our bodies.

sperm
Tiny specks of life even smaller than a woman's egg. They are present in a milky liquid called semen that men produce. Sperm is needed to fertilise a woman's eggs.

tummy
Many people call the part of the body below the chest the tummy. The tummy also means the stomach, which digests food, and this gets squashed a little as the womb and baby grow in size.

vitamins
Substances that we need in our diet but only in small amounts.

womb
The place inside a woman's body where a baby can grow and develop.

Further information
WEBSITES
www.bbc.co.uk/science/ humanbody/body
A website with games and interactive information about the human body.

www.kidshealth.org
Information about your body. Click on the section called 'for kids'.

www.sciencemuseum.org.uk exhibitions/lifecycle/index.asp
A website from the Science Museum in London that looks at the human life-cycle.

www.bbc.co.uk/parenting/ your_kids
This BBC website has lots of information about how children grow and develop.

Note to parents and teachers: Every effort has been made by the Publishers to ensure that these websites are suitable for children, that they are of the highest educational value, and that they contain no inappropriate or offensive material. However, because of the nature of the Internet, it is impossible to guarantee that the contents of these sites will not be altered. We strongly advise that Internet access is supervised by a responsible adult.

Index

These are the lists of contents for each title in *Your Body - Inside and Out*

Bones and Muscles

Under your skin • Your skeleton • Body armour • Joints • Fingers and thumbs • Shoulders and hips • Your neck • Your spine • Muscles move your bones • Moving your elbow • Exercise • Moving your face • Breaks and sprains

Food and Digestion

Food is fuel • Energy foods: starches • Energy foods: sugars • Body-building foods • Fats and oils • Fruit and vegetables • What happens to food? • Chew and swallow • Into the intestines • Absorbing food • Water and waste • Problems with foods • A healthy diet

Growing

The cycle of life • Producing babies • Inside the womb • Everyone is different • A newborn baby • From six months to one year old • Toddlers • From toddler to child • Young children • From child to adult • Fully grown • Getting older • Keeping healthy

Heart and Lungs

The heart and lungs • The heart is a muscle • The heart is a pump • What is blood for? • We need oxygen • Your ribs move • Lungs are sponges • Gases in and out • The blood system • The four-part heart • A healthy heart • Strong heart and lungs • Checking your pulse

Senses

What are the senses? • Your brain • Seeing • Inside the eye • Wearing glasses • Hearing • Inside your eye • Hard of hearing • Smelling • Tasting • Touching • Heat and pain • Working together

Teeth and Hair

Looking good • What are teeth made of? • Shapes of teeth • Two sets of teeth • Cleaning teeth • Stronger and straighter • Tooth decay • What causes tooth decay? • How hair grows • Protecting your skin • Looking after hair • Head lice • Treating head lice